How Naked

the

Loneliness

By

Philip Butera

Philip Butera

JaCol Publishing Inc.
Copyright 2025 © by JaCol Publishing Inc.
Illustrations Copyright © 2025
by JaCol Publishing Inc.
FIRST PRINTING
March 2025
All rights reserved
JaCol Publishing Inc.
195 Murica Aisle
Irvine, CA 92614
818-510-2898
Editor-in-Chief: Randall
Andrews
www.jacolpublishing.com
ISBN:

Cover artwork: GS Harper
gsharperinspirations@gmail.com
Cover design: Christopher Moore
christophercmoore@gmail.com
This book is dedicated to Diane

Foreword

I cannot honestly account for how long I have known
Philip. My logical mind tells me it has been only a few
years; my visceral mind tells me I have always known
him. We met under the most ordinary of circumstances.
Philip came into my print shop, looking to have some
pages of one of his books printed and help design a cover
for another. We instantly found a mutual respect and
artistic connection. Before long, he had invited me to
perform in a podcast of his book "Caught Between,"
which is based on actual events in the 1970s. He even
found a way in the script to explain why my Tennessee
accent was in a New York City crime drama.

During these collaborations on the mechanics of
making a book, I came to know Philip's gift with the
nuance of phrase, the entrainment of emotion and
meaning, and the dedication to Flaubert's "le mot juste."
A true renaissance man of the arts, Philip turns his
prodigious talents to prose, poetry, plays, and more. His
words always find their mark, whether the reader's heart
or intellect, with precision and deftness.

He has referred to this latest volume, "How Naked
The Loneliness," as "his bloodletting." And, in many
ways, it is just that. A highly personal dive into the
meaning of life, love, sadness, joy, and meaning, this
compelling long-form poetry exhilarates and exhausts

Philip Butera

the reader while leaving a hunger to consume it
repeatedly. You will find yourself reading... thinking...
rereading... rethinking.

Christopher Moore

Graphic Artist, Designer, Author

Testimonials

"The sheer talent and skill of Philip Butera as a writer simply cannot be disputed. He is a language wizard when using the written word to present imagery, ideas, and feelings that are profound yet easily absorbed by the reader. Additionally, if poetry is meant to be read aloud, Butera's work is satisfying indeed."

Salvatore Alessi, Adjunct Professor of Literature, Canisius College

"Philip Butera uses words and phrases like an accomplished artist uses color and light. Excellent balance of imagery and abstraction. His command of language is broad and lush."

Nicole Washburn, Editor, Ghostwriter

"Philip Butera writes incredible poems. His vibrant language and artistic visions will have you clamoring for more."

Ann Christine Tabaka, Multi-Award-Winning Poet

"Philip Butera glides, rides, manipulates, caresses, seduces, and inhibits language. While his images and phrasing initially appear complex and constant, he manages to be clear and concise with both. To call him anything short of a verbal

4

Philip Butera

genius would be a denial of his unparalleled ownership of the richest of all languages."

Kathleen Bryce Niles, Editor, Comstock Review

"With raw passion and profound psychological perception, Philip's poetry pierces your innermost being."

Eva E. A. Skoe, Ph.D., Clinical Psychology, Professor of Psychology

Philip Butera

Note from the Author:

I had been in Italy for three weeks and decided to travel north and take a twelve-day cruise in the Baltic Sea. I had never been to Estonia, Finland, or Sweden. The cruise ship, the Celebrity Apex, was large, and I would say it had a near-capacity of just under 3,000 passengers.

I was alone and observed my fellow passengers aboard the ship and on excursions. I watched their behaviors. There were mostly couples, some with children of varying ages. Primarily Americans but other nationalities as well. Mainly people over fifty.

After a few days, I realized I wasn't noticing - I was studying my fellow passengers. I watched facial expressions, body language, tone of voice, how they dressed, and how couples interacted. What I identified was how clearly their discontent was exposed.

We were on a grand ship with full accommodations and everything that could be desired, yet most couples were lonely, and that loneliness was visible. Their yearnings and weariness of being were evident in their mannerisms and demeanor. I whispered to myself, *"How naked the Loneliness?"* That phrase would not leave my thoughts for the cruise, and I decided it would be the perfect title for my next poetry book.

Philip M. Butera

Philip Butera

Contents

Another Fall

The weight once more
from another fall.
A mixture
of woeful emotions
raging.

This burden of tears
nourishing the despair
that cruelly,
holds me
captive.

Deep neglected wounds
thicken into scars.
Sorrow becoming
a relentless
bell tolling.

I AM disillusionment,
held in flesh,
contained in life.

My thoughts screaming

as I descend

into

hopelessness.

Again,

once more

the anguish

of another,

another

fall.

Philip Butera

Cottony Clouds

The winds of winter push

cottony clouds

before the moon

in the dark of night.

I remain,

missing more pieces

than I can gather.

The air is numbing cold

and my shadow

has

disappeared into

frozen snowdrifts.

January

is an unforgiving month,

like

a lover in distress

who sacrifices

reality for a dream.

Philip Butera

There are always doubts

about

whether great love

equals great pain.

There are always doubts.

I am nostalgic and yearning

for the warmth

of an afternoon sun.

I long for summer.

I long for July,

lovely July

when

I was whole

and your smile

danced before me.

I remember the heat

and I remember

the crisp white sheets.

I was that lover

Philip Butera

who sought

but never saw.

5

Flawed

Orchids are delicate,

a passion,

an obsession.

Roses are appropriate

for love

or death.

The Buttercup is overlooked

and the Easter Lily

is always acting

to entice you.

Know

that I love lilacs.

They are not bashful.

They announce their presence

even before being seen.

I am careful or careless

depending on one's

definition.

Simply self-assured or selfish,

depending on my mood.

Flowers are intriguing images,

like a dazzling ring on a finger

or a glowing branding iron

about to touch your heart.

Lost thoughts gather

among the clouds

and then disappear

when the Sun

breaks through.

That same Sun

that nourishes flowers,

turns them pale yellow

and

brittle around the edges.

I can't seem to grasp my actions,

I love,

I lose.

I buy flowers

they die.

I once had dreams

but they were flawed

often centered

on sight and scent.

Picture me in a garden

surrounded

by beautiful flowers

celebrating summer.

I was among the Tulips

and

unprepared for

the wrecking ball

about to

smash

into my desires.

Philip Butera

It only took

a few words

and what was colorful and stunning

and what was not

became questionable and gray.

Leaden gray.

Gray, the blush

of no garden.

I notice Marigolds now.

Golden Marigolds.

They are polite

not intrusive.

They give one permission

to see beyond

what is staring

past them.

Philip Butera

In an Affair, the Brush Barely Touches the Canvas

At dawn,

before breakfast,

before the indulgence, the words, and the aftermath

I needed the truth.

That slippery serpent that chokes and discards.

You smiled thinly,

"Perceive what you will," you said, "I need to shower."

He was wealthy, and I was a pair of dark glasses you
wore occasionally.

He purchased, and I shopped.

A light burns, and a light's shadow blends.

Color, texture, and shape describe a work of art.

In a relationship,

the foreground is devoured, and the background is
lyrical.

In an affair,

the brush barely touches the canvas, and other narratives
become possibilities.

Naked and obedient,

you are borrowed like fine art exhibited from gallery to
gallery.

Gran Sasso, Italy, became a fist to the chest

as the clouds turned dark,

the heavy rains started, while your scent lingered

on the sheets and in my thoughts.

Fine glass

is never used to secure.

It is to be admired, handled, and then put away.

If dropped, by chance or purpose,

a momentary visual experience

is created

before the chards are swept into a heap

and then discarded.

You were cold and self-absorbed

when you hurried out the door.

I leaned back on the bedroom chair

tapped the tips of my fingers together

and eventually closed my eyes.

Excuses were a credit I believed I deserved.

Philip Butera

Though I understood
how optimism
usually morphs into a sad smile.

You are an illusionist
and your carefully crafted illusion
makes the truth
an uncertainty that chimes
silently and deadly.

Your note
had no inhibitions.
It stood there propped against an empty wine glass.
Your handwriting was graceful, stylish, and to the point.
"Forever was never on my mind."

Philip Butera

More Shadow Than Cause

Athena realized intimacy was
just moonlight in a cage.

When I make a mistake, I dwell and dwell
and dwell.
I lie to myself,
saying, "None of us are free from weakness."
Sadness is a descent without limits,
without a foundation
to land upon.

Apollo became a hawk
with razor-sharp talons.

I live in a space where light and dark overlap.
Where disenchantment spirals indelicately
and mystery confounds.
There is a somber restlessness inside me,
a disquieting illusion,
a banished panther, more shadow than cause

Philip Butera

inhabiting where
nightmares are echoes
of selves to be.

Because of her beauty,

Aphrodite was the most hated of all the Gods.

Silence can't be cunning,

it struggles with self-definition.

Heartbeats are only a refrain,

and this

blankness

stresses comprehension.

Comfortable in pretense

is my survival quilt

for

I am always what has been

never what remains.

Sad Music

Helplessly masquerading,

spilling spontaneous plots

from a mournful stream of revision

I remain

without transformation

in an age of light

seduced by darkness.

Acting creates a person,

personality betrays the reflection

and

devoid of boundaries

memories become afterthoughts

of more memories

with

more memories yet to come.

In an awakened dream

froth with quicksand vices

sad music

underscores

the

tragedy.

If tragedy still has a definition

or is it

just a word on a marquee

directed by metaphors

and produced

in spite

of Freud and Huxley.

Expect invitations

to a trial and error

wasteland.

Your choice,

contemp for my questions

or

applause

for Cain's transgressions.

Philip Butera

Disenchanted With Illusions

I am

mad from thinking.

Disenchanted with illusions

I pace my mind

but

dreams interrupt dreaming.

Memories become

ellipses,

thoughts harangue.

I cling

to me,

a cataclysm,

in spiraling descent,

distracted

only

by nightmares.

Philip Butera

The Albatross With Muddy Feet

Persistent sleep

suits me,

the long, relentless-

solitude.

I am comfortable between a void and an abyss.

Once the actor –

adored by his image

now, my reveries,

hover above what's abandoned.

A battered collage of memories

is an afterglow of pretense

from a fall to elusive to alter.

Nothing is ever

as real

as a nightmare

in a stranger's bed.

The Albatross with muddy feet,

though engaging,

is little more than

a lingering promise from an unremembered dream.

His arrogance a recklessness–

a hunger

for an anticipated tryst.

Grooming himself

to impress a white Dove

his weight drew him into

the swells.

Safe from hope, without desires,

sleep is restful.

Yet, at times,

the warmth of being

occupies my thoughts.

The bird has disappeared.

The setting has changed,

but the tragedy,

remains.

Philip Butera

A Miss at Twilight

They were called marbles.

They were called reasons.

I am never where I am

when I need to be.

When "I'm sorry" is necessary

or "I'm leaving" is the only response.

I fear life is destructible

and consolation

is a round-trip ticket

to go round and round.

It's in your eyes.

Your eyes looking into mine.

Counterfeit glances

through a snow globe,

leaving tiny droplets

behind on the surface,

soon to gather and stain.

Philip Butera

Gather and stain.

Suffering

is a repeatable offense,

a language

the soul whispers to the heart

on a dark, lonely night,

with darker contemplation

to come.

To gather and stain.

Broken and repellant

in a bookstore

that sells small bags of marbles

I see

Cats' eyes and beauties.

Tragedy radiates from them,

they have no function,

except to be.

Except to be.

Philip Butera

Reason teaches us

that

to be completely forgotten

is to climb into ourselves

and be put

in another's pocket.

I am a miss at twilight.

At dawn

I separate myself from the chasm.

Somewhere in between

you have a thought of me

and I tremble

involuntarily

like

a visitor

at a cemetery.

Philip Butera

Unremarkable

Nowhere is an outlet for assurance.

A valley of simplicity

to soothe the hollowness inside.

No guide or provider,

just a narrow pathway

to separate myself from the stage

I wake up upon every morning.

I am a performer

pretending to be aware

but always with the urge

of faltering

and revealing the absence

of who you believe

I am.

Unremarkable,

is a solitary term,

Philip Butera

a polite light without a probe.

It is a weak grasp,

cultivated

for a tedious performance

again

and again,

over and over.

I am both a tear and a step

in and out of the main frame.

A non-glossy enigma

frightened

when silhouettes

are analyzed

and found to be a refuge

for well-being.

We don't say prayers,

those of us

riddled with the consequences

of knowing illusion and life

Philip Butera

occur on a precipice

of our own making.

We wish to disappear,

disappear from the realm

where accepting

what we endure

is a constant,

where desire hides

the shadow of composing

an articulate

but sad

suicide note.

Philip Butera

Seduce and Embrace

These feelings

are self-medicating,

neither truth

nor wisdom.

Just

psychological intrigue

with comic interludes.

How cunning,

the absence of significance.

Those emotional calamities

accountable

to neither God nor

his interpreters.

You and I,

naked

and illuminated

spread wide

Philip Butera

what few can understand,

that hope unmasked

is tedious in perspective.

We,

you and I

have moments

when our new selves

are remembered

by our old selves.

How uncanny

to be loathed

and yet attract

those

who sacrifice delight for reality.

To seduce and embrace

is a bold stride

from those of us

confident enough

to rely upon intimacy

27

Philip Butera

for absolution.

A closeness those

who prefer to float

rather

than dive,

consider impetuous.

I call you

an act of force

with a passing smile

running a wet crimson finger

across

pleasurable crimes

yet to be committed.

Once aware,

dreaming and imagination

fuels fluid cleverness,

bringing out the darkest of gazes,

from an audience

Philip Butera

devoid

of cultural discontent

and feeling

vacantly unremorseful.

Philip Butera

There Is No Now

April, May, and June are the names of lovers.

July is threadbare blue and lacks curiosity.

September captures our attention.

The other months lack notoriety except for January.

A month that is never humble

and uses irony to express itself.

Slaughterhouse-Five bounded from Brave New World

but few noticed.

I did.

Though illogical, there is no now,

the drawbridges, love, and religion

have prompted a world without feeling.

The past marrying what will be

has eliminated the need

for now.

Human nature

is counterintuitive

and

purpose has become purposeful.

Purposeful

is such a nice word.

Exposition may be needed

but without a now.

It is redundant.

On a dull evening, while I watched stars attempting to

caress,

my fantasies crept forward to invade my thoughts,

but in my absence, the absurdity of life

became a realty

and forgiveness became self-sacrifice.

There are no rebels left,

just coffee grounds that clog the drain.

I can't say I overlooked the mask of rage

I was simply in this era.

This period.

There were no introductions, not even an invitation.

A waterfall of apathy had cleansed us from brooding.

Philip Butera

Predators disguised as Apostles

caused scarlet red to saturate all virtues.

Anything was better than waiting,

waiting for the months to drool into long or short days.

Anything to break apart into *any* and *thing*,

as long as it was visual

and could be

a moveable feast when

words were discarded

and the volume turned up.

My girlfriend had said to her friends,

 "I was her mistress."

If you were born in March,

that is the way you spoke,

with a *marching* cadence without interest or care.

They occupied a mirage of thought

and chuckled at compassion.

There were no riddles in March,

just damp, heavy winds.

When asked for details

Philip Butera

My girlfriend exclaimed, "I noted the themes of Dickens

and found them lacking in distinction."

Like "nothing" in neon,

she, too, was a merchant.

Flight connections were crucial.

Notifications were broadcast

on screens with operative intelligence.

When leaving for a place identical

to your departure,

arrivals are always on time.

No one was missed, and no one strayed

or was seen with bloodied hands.

There were no blue-eyed servant girls,

only innocent bystanders who were guilty

of using a bread knife when a gun

was more appropriate.

Death was entirely sentimentalized

in homespun musicals

where the hero was absent,

Philip Butera

the anti-hero unaware

and the villains, unnamed.

They were applauded rather than understood.

Most received the Undistinguished Service Cross

with honors.

So, the Sun gradually discovered its true identity,

the idea of seasons began to weaken

and

the favor of time, with its unlimited obstruction

becomes the opposite

of what its meaning once was.

No one cared,

though pets became scarce.

I realized

it's not like it ever goes away,

after all, I was born in January

it all made sense.

Numbers were used as fillers

and

Philip Butera

quips as filters.

Off the fading pages in the far distance,

I recalled, remembering

Stardust

the song and the reality

and I guessed,

Wanda saved the Savage,

Miss Havisham seduced Pip

and Mrs. Dalloway,

understanding the purity of happiness

killed herself.

Philip Butera

When the Moon Whispered Through the Clouds

When the moon

whispered through the clouds

she responded

with a kiss.

Tired

but wide awake

we lay on the soft grass

beneath the willow tree

close to the water's edge.

Her skin, the color of white roses

and her lips, pale pink.

My arm, around her neck,

holding her close.

She was relaxed,

one naked leg over mine.

Yet, I can never be in the moment,

any moment.

Philip Butera

I never feel the moment.

Always

on to the next, on to the next

to moments,

safe and empty.

Days became weeks

until the chime of late Autumn

held the willow tree naked.

Certainty is the answer

to an unasked question

Certainty never suited me.

It is a trick,

layered and compacted,

creating a disquieting result.

She cut her hair,

changed her style,

and ties to me.

Never in the moment,

Philip Butera

purpose lacks influence.

I smiled a vacant smile

and went to the uncomfortable,

A place that welcomed

the cold.

Familiar with thoughts,

instead of deeds

I stood at the water's edge

peering at my rippling reflection,

pretending to

remember her name.

The Woman I Need

I am as seaweed on a stone

either clinging from the last pass of water

or anticipating riding

on the next wave.

I am a silhouette of myself at times.

Burdened

with modern unforgiveness,

holding my hand over

a candle burning

through

one day from another.

If one is to dream

love is an extravagance,

yearned

from the bedroom

while

experiencing

the cold nights of winter.

I can feel the seams

losing strength.

An allusion

bearing the solemnity

of difficult questions

I ask myself.

And music

provokes reminiscences,

devoid

of a predicate.

What remains

are

desire's

bittersweet

scars.

Experiences,

are dangerous grounds,

Philip Butera

abandoning oneself,

abandoning

what is necessary

to understand

tragedy's consequences

or

contradiction's demands.

I

yearn to foresee,

to weave a net

across

the enigmas

and dissipate

the contrived

influences.

There is a pier

where beneath,

the waves splash in rhymes.

Every Sunday at dusk

Philip Butera

a woman

with long brown hair

stands at the furthest end

and smiles

every time a cat

strolls along the

guardrail.

I lose interest in myself,

watching that woman,

that woman.

That woman

is the woman

I need.

Philip Butera

The Distance is a Spiral Refusing to be Undone

I am not
the mirror's image
confident and smiling,
I am behind
that silvery illusion
locked in contradiction,

I am
a gliding contour
among masks of indifference.
Stitched together
with a confluence of missteps.

I am neither whole
nor mad
but a curious intruder
vexed by my reflection.

If you attempt to hold me,
or comfort me
you will stumble.
Others have.
Still, others
beaming with confidence
watched
as the storm had gathered.

All of them realized,
some too late,

Philip Butera

that my tragedy
was
connected
to a cloudy place
of clarity.
A place of reckoning.

When you are
loved by someone
looking for themselves
they lack an expanse of time
and are
unaware
that the distance
is a spiral
refusing to be
undone.

I hear crows caw,
as if born into anger.
I feel the void
inside
clawing for more space
and even
when you are near
I see a reflection
that prefers
to be
alone.

Philip Butera

Clawing and Crawling

Soft and kind

are

felt in another variation

when

waves confine ambition.

I can't find what is under,

under

the many variables

hidden

under the fabric,

when the fabric

itself is hidden

under

a fabricated

lifestyle.

There are many reasons to cry.

When you lose a lover

Philip Butera

who was a friend

but

the intimacy is missed

not the closeness.

Purpose and destruction

seek

comfort

from reasoning.

Problems

which serve deceit well

come to mind.

There are scars across the eyes,

across the miles

and though merit

is sacrificed for appearance

you can hear

the laughter from those

who know you.

Philip Butera

I

am an actor,

and by no means

a dancer.

I

yield vicariously

to sermons

and

pretend to come alive.

I

have found

the womb of the soul

favors

deception

and

it is easier to demand

than to

take notice.

To gamble with God,

know that

Philip Butera

the devil wins.

You must

fall to your knees

clawing and crawling,

until

a voice inside your head

screams,

"Just wake up."

Philip Butera

An Antecedent

No longer telltale signs.

There are terms we have borrowed,

others we have adopted.

Some say there is a process.

Others, a capacity.

I have a disdain for luck.

That potent

but fleeting sense of occurrence.

Fate is either arrogance or insecurity.

An invitation to change,

multiplying uncertainties.

False illusions are

never false to the interpreter.

They are the weight

of acceptance.

There are sculptors

Philip Butera

of consciousness.

Their hands are free

to provoke another

and another.

To lace

an imagined afterglow

beforehand

and

abandon apprehension.

We forget

that images interpret life.

Art is a reflection of the now,

never the past.

There is a dread of healing.

A dread of reflections

turning cold

and the knowledge

that life

is always on the verge

never

Philip Butera

on the rebound.

I have a fluttering of expressions

when there is an inaccuracy

in discerning.

How the horrific is disguised

by the numbing

of hooks

deepening.

I see a man

in a white shirt

wearing a wedding band

sitting on a bench.

He's busily shaping a rope.

He's going to hang himself.

He's disillusioned with what remains

when certainty

is confiscated.

As the rope snakes over a sturdy oak branch

and falls to him

he realizes

his life,

that life

is an antecedent

not even modifying a proper noun

just highlighting

a simple

forgettable

pronoun.

Philip Butera

Plowed Pathways

Caution,

a conceptual formula

fraught with

contingencies

creeps noiselessly

toward the front

of my mind.

I am a tragedy

sailing

from the facts

that distinguish

manner from value.

My tears

are hidden

under contradictions,

I cannot

undress from myself.

Philip Butera

I am a believer

in myths,

wistful yet grand.

But believing

has become luminous,

a target

for vultures.

Have you glanced at the screens?

The plowed pathways

expressing volumes

too loud to hear.

Where truth

has been exiled

to a grating cacophony

of emptiness,

portrayed

from

fools wearing masks.

The weight of weightlessness

Philip Butera

is capricious

and that failure of imagination

creates self-deception.

I hear, *let it be*

but

let it be

only leads

to a roar of confinement.

How quaint to reflect

and ponder the allegory

when Homer and Hamlet

were a tremble

voided in youth

and now

eloquence

is noted as

deadly words

on black banners.

Intelligent, bright eyes

Philip Butera

recognize

a honied rapture,

blossoming

while others

with dulled vision

relinquish

awareness

for

indelicate enthusiasm.

Philip Butera

The Death of Disappearance

Beautiful Annabel Lee set up her easel

aside from the blaze of Vesuvius.

Angels dripped paint

on her palette.

Flutes and strings

so ethereal

a dawn of colors awakened

with a glistening texture

both flames and lava

envied.

But a telling wind

from a restless sea

darkened the splendor,

reminding artists

they were only cinders

yet to be consumed

by their creations.

While I sipped Limoncello

Philip Butera

Gauguin told me,

"Van Gogh was gone."

"Why?" I asked.

> *Without emotion*
>
> *he pointed toward*
>
> *Annabel Lee's easel.*

Dead characters

in jumpsuits

from stories

I was willing but hadn't read,

began appearing in the sky.

Those that

were awakened by their

descending

swore they would

never live again.

Changing time was not desirable

though the nostalgia

for light and shadow

woven into tragedy was.

Philip Butera

Those with deep secrets

admired

every brush stroke

Annabel Lee

added to her canvas.

Lady Macbeth

loved my laugh.

She stood on her bed,

discarding

her royal costume.

Her slim, winter-pink body

preferred pleasure over reason's protests.

My soft brown eyes viewed her cold blue ones

from the moistness between her legs.

Our motive

in Annabel Lee's eyes

was neither deceptive nor opportunistic

but

the answer

to an unasked question.

Philip Butera

I had had her before,

in a novel

Christopher Marlowe

was yet to write.

We agreed at a gambling table in a brothel.

I will always be

the intellectual

who never accomplished

anything but thinking.

$\qquad$ *Lady Macbeth*

$\qquad$ *would be*

$\qquad$ *all things that could not be explained*

$\qquad$ *after the tip of Annabel Lee's brush*

$\qquad$ *left her palette.*

I met

Elvis Presley

in a raven-shaped Jacuzzi.

He was singing

"The Weight"

Philip Butera

when Oswald

shot him.

A chilling gust came from

behind a cloud

directing me past

the path where

the death of disappearance

with incentives to remain

was an illusion

not for transforming

but repeating,

the weight, the weight

again

and again.

That was the reason

why Annabel Lee

chose her

colors

carefully.

As my mind burned,

Philip Butera

I danced with memories

of the girls from my youth.

>*The redhead with clear green eyes*

>*woke us,*

>*Annabel Lee and me.*

I smiled

at her unfinished canvas,

there were women

all reminiscent of Lady Macbeth

grabbing at my thoughts.

Feeling fraudulent,

I replaced my heart

with sentences

full of meaning.

Every artist

moving in the direction

of obsession

knew the treasure not grasped

was called madness

not

Philip Butera

the accepted

gambit of

scorpions mating.

Annabel Lee's

narrative

was to have us un-disbelieve.

Leaving the kingdom by the sea,

I followed

another Lady Macbeth.

The one,

everyone called "stunning."

We walked into

The Pit and the Pendulum

where those who loved

imprudently

stepped forward

to greet us.

With each swing

expectation

beckoned

Philip Butera

in the darkness.

> *Annabel Lee spoke softly*
>
> *as her brush was set aside,*
>
> *"Alone inside once,*
>
> *and nevermore."*

I understood immediately.

> *Annabel Lee's*
>
> *self-portrait*
>
> *was*
>
> *my image-*
>
> *Lady Macbeth,*
>
> *steeped in honeyed-sepia*
>
> *naked and pleased.*

Philip Butera

Inevitability

Inevitability
is the word
that disguises the rage
we feel
deeply inside
us.

It is deception,
but
scars and bitterness
remain.
They weaken
yet remain.

Inevitability
is the melody
of a dance
expected.
But not
without guilt.

Philip Butera

Did You Know Hades Had Three Levels

Expectation,

is the erosion of reason

while

inadequacy matures.

She said, grinning, "Did you know Hades had three levels?"

An optimist might comment

on the boundless fruits of the heart,

how the purity of mind

casts off the uneasiness

of where one will travel.

I answered sourly, "It makes no difference once you die."

She asked, "Do you believe in forgiveness?"

There are determinations

and limitations.

Storms that devour

extravagant yearnings.

One

must be mindful of consequences.

I looked out the picture window at the snow

gently falling underneath the streetlight.

Philip Butera

My youth came to mind,
my mother baking cookies
that smell of warming strawberry jam.

The house was immaculate except
for the floor mat at the front door
where everyone stomped their feet
to rid themselves of their sins.

The snow was gathering,
and that stirred something inside me.
Neither bold nor innocent
just a notion of moving on.
A feeling of stripping myself of me
and freeing some
entanglement
that has been trapped
inside for a while.

There is nothing to compare
nothing with.
Intimacy is either
the appetizer or the dessert,
never the main course.
Never what fills you up.

Philip Butera

Never what unlocks mysteries.

It is a pleasant paralysis,

thoroughly remorseless

and

pallid upon appeal.

She somehow looked less pleasing,

less attractive to me

or maybe

it was me less attractive to myself.

Her delicate features hardened, "Deceiving yourself is the
scented vapor you adore being blessed with."

The snow continued to fall

all evening

with little sign of letting up.

Philip Butera

Pain is a Creative Experience

Pain

is a creative experience.

It's an immersion

into dampened illusions

and

derelict gashes.

Try to subjugate

remorse,

try to subjugate

distress.

Pretentiousness

then

appears

to subjugate

the deadliest of all serpents,

objectivity,

the bonding

agent

between man and man.

Garlands

and impetuousness

are needed

to restrain awareness.

A venerable soot on sanity

is executed.

A fragile operation

deftly applied

with a hammer and a lie.

Artists see peaceful stillness

as a target

to struggle with self-definition.

The accomplishment

being an admission,

an admiration

of guilt.

Lines and contours

dreamily

function

as the mediation

between voice

and sentiment.

I have reveled

in disappointment.

I have put a razor to my wrists

But I have never

corralled my thoughts

to sing in harmony

with what has been kneaded and hewn

to justify

what isn't

for what is.

Philip Butera

My Friend Hears Music When She Dreams

My friend hears music

when she dreams.

There are no boundaries,

just sounds to glide upon.

It is all dimensions,

a warm yellow

bathing

in a rainbow.

In my dreams

I am running barefoot

on glass and gravel

to escape

from a stranger chasing me,

gaining on me.

There are no margins,

just

scarlet edges

being swallowed

by darkness.

Philip Butera

I try to dream

about metaphors

born of opportunities.

But there are no opportunities

in dreams.

Only fading recollections

and

puzzling imagery.

My friend sees music in her dreams,

a cavalcade

of all things meaningful.

In my dreams,

I brood on what relentless means.

It seeps into my faults

and turns me

toward

a beckoning sea.

Philip Butera

A Child's Kiss to an Ill Wind

Processional songs with preconditions

but no contemplative insight

are about provocation, not transformation.

People chanting

becoming indistinguishable from stage characters

dismissing the morality

of a consequence.

There are rhetorical glances

when metaphors produce hooves

and

intention becomes an accepted probe

for those who believe duplicity

is a desirable variable

to cascade a swarm.

Philip Butera

When reason and fear collide,

self-deception

objectifies

ridicule and scorn.

Weakness inclines to pale

when luminous.

I have created abstract poetry

when stoned.

Criticized bad poets

while drinking

but I never

mistook a stunning rhapsody

for

a glazed social contingency.

There is no harm in being a dreamer

even when the trigger

of analogy is just an impression

of a lost cause.

Peace and love

have

dried and crumbled,

becoming just a wisp,

a child's kiss

to an ill wind.

What is the evolution of drama?

Consider the image

of an armoire without mystery.

Nothing exists gratuitously

except for deceit

and

the cold eyes of a loved one

as their dagger

is being withdrawn.

Philip Butera

I Hear Demons Laugh

I despise this reflection,

the desperation in my eyes

and

hostility in my thoughts.

I imagine the slice of a knife.

Blood, leave quickly.

Stop trickling,

just gush

and be drained.

Cuffed to emotions,

I hear demons laugh.

They laugh,

and they laugh,

coating my thoughts with gloom.

77

Philip Butera

Expectations

fracture into icy fragments

that

circle my heart.

Vipers gather

in dreams

not yet dreamt.

I replace my shadow

with myself

oblivious to explanations

about

never quite finding

the vanishing line

between

accomplice and visionary.

Uncomfortable,

Philip Butera

now

with these masks

I have worn,

hang me out in the cold,

beneath the moonlight.

Where the wolves

hunt for easy prey.

Philip Butera

No Longer a Crusader for Antiquity's Heaven

I am

mad from thinking,

mad from being.

Disenchanted with illusions

and

tired of delusions.

I pace my mind,

at the edge

where elusive predators,

await

in the dim light, disappearing

almost,

almost,

capturing my attention.

One dream interrupts another.

Distant images become

thinning ellipses,

Philip Butera

tempering

the language of awakening.

Desire and sorrow

spills

from a quaint landscape

into a ghostly imperfection

on a canvas

unreachable.

No longer

a crusader

for antiquity's heaven.

I cling to myself,

a scream,

in whirling descent

distracted

only by

sobering madness.

Philip Butera

One of Those That the Sea Beckons

My tears

cloud the storm

as I dream away,

holding myself

captive.

Again,

another descent.

It is only time that separates

the wounds

from the scars.

Yet again,

that choir

of anguish

adds flames

Philip Butera

to thoughts.

I am,

one of those

that the sea beckons

with a profound eloquence.

Though

I scream for belief,

the waves rush

hurriedly

toward me.

Philip Butera

Tragedy is a Parasitic Creature Whose Prey is Passion

Contentment

is a half-moral cheerlessness

that numbs

what is uncomfortable.

There is an unattainable

idyllic inclination

that we accomplish

by disbelieving

because expressing is easier

than becoming.

How quaint

to defy all the risks

in feelings,

while

Philip Butera

accepting the condemnation

of thinking.

We have creativity,

devised,

a fundamentally flawed

distinction

between passage and passing.

One is death

and the other

is admitting one is dead.

Not literally

of course

but figuratively.

A lack of clarity

is unpitying,

insidious in its refrain

of helplessness.

Philip Butera

Accepted helplessness.

Welcomed

helplessness.

Tragedy is a parasitic creature

whose prey is passion

but whose

intoxication

is

idealistic perfection.

I own guns.

I own books.

Both have

fearful

expectations.

I understand the difference between

what is borrowed

Philip Butera

and what is asked for.

I know time

is silent

and what is pleasant

is a ruse,

a disguise to tame peril.

Yet,

a beautiful illusion

is never seen

as a

divine comedy.

Philip Butera

Biography

Books by

Philip M. Butera

Poetry:

Mirror Images and Shards of Glass
Dark Images at Sea
I Never finished Loving You
Falls from Grace, Favor & High Places
Forever was Never on my Mind

Novels:
Caught Between
Art and Mystery: The Lost Poe Manuscript
Far From Here

Artbooks:
Breathing Life into Thought

Plays:
The Apparition
The Poet's Masque
Happier Than Madness